The experiences of fifteen workers, from the 40's to the present day

Published by Gatehouse Books Ltd, Hulme Adult Education Centre, Stretford Road, Manchester M15 5FQ.

Gatehouse is grateful for continued financial support from Manchester City Council and North West Arts Board, and for financial assistance for the production of this book from The Paul Hamlyn Foundation, The Manchester Guardian Society Trust, The Publications Editorial Group (PEG). PEG funding towards the production of this book came from a fund established in the late 1980s in the Inner London Education Authority Community Education branch. The fund aimed to promote the publishing of critical reflection on adult and community education by practitioners. This publication is one of the final projects to be funded. All the money is now spent.

Gatehouse is grateful for continuing support from Manchester Adult Education Services.

Gatehouse would like to thank the members of the Working Lives book selection group from Spurley Hey Adult Education Centre: Pauline Brennan, Chris Hayes, Muriel Gilbertson, Joanne Howard, Janice Mearman, Janice McNeive, Angela Millington, Pauline Sergeant, Hazel Shaw, Maura Sweeney, Elaine Wood.

Thanks also to groups run by Manchester Adult Education Services at Greenheys Centre, Varna Centre and Longsight Library who commented on an early draft of the book.

Illustrations: Jenny Bowers pages 22,41,45,49; Caroline Jariwala pages 17,81,85,93; Rick Blakely page 34.

Photographs, Mick Clarke

Book design, David Andrassy

Editor, Patricia Duffin

Printed by Manchester Free Press

Line breaking

We have designed this book
to make it useful to people
who don't find reading easy.
Some stories
are broken into short lines like this,
so you can take a break
at a point that makes sense.

Contents

Introduction

This book brings together the experiences of 15 workers, stretching from the 40's to the present day. They write about the fears of that first day at work; the excitement of making new friends and developing new skills; the struggle to manage caring for children with going out to work. For some there is the pride of achievement: of becoming a chargewoman; starting a business; being recognised as a right hand man. For others, their working life has been marked by illness, redundancy, stress and appalling work conditions. Among the voices are those who have come to work here from other countries. Their collective voices present a picture of the working lives of many in the second half of the twentieth century.

Each writer gives us also some insight into how they came into education and how they came to write about work.

A lot of people were involved in putting this book together. Among them was a group of ten basic skills students and their tutor from Spurley Hey Centre, in Manchester. They worked with Gatehouse to read, discuss and then select these stories from all those submitted. Their initial concern was whether they were capable of doing this.

"Who are we to criticise somebody else's work? Could we really do it? Should we do it?" *Angela*

However, as they met and worked together, week after week, they found themselves caught up in these stories by ordinary people.

"So, it gives you the inspiration that maybe you could do it as well." *Pauline S.*

They found also that changes were happening to them.

"My confidence has improved because we've had group discussions and I've done work for it towards Wordpower Stage II*." *Janice Mc.*

"I've been very surprised with myself because I didn't think I could have an insight like I have done with a few of the things." *Pauline B.*

They gradually became aware of the challenge of saying No.

"The first couple of meetings I was actually frightened of saying No and I sat and listened to everyone else to see what they'd say but as the weeks went on I got a bit of confidence." *Pauline B.*

In the end, they decided:

"We've gained a skill, haven't we? It's all to our benefit. Number one, working as a group, participating, communicating and acting together. The other one is looking at different styles of writing and being able to take bits out, and to be constructive in our criticism. Because although we say things we didn't like, we say why we didn't like it or we give alternative things that could be put in." *Pauline S.*

**City and Guilds certificate*

Their tutor, Chris Hayes, sees it as being significant that they were already a well-established group, comfortable in opening up to each other.

"We're not afraid to speak out. Everybody knew what other people were capable of saying." *Maura*

We hope that this book will encourage you to talk and write with others.

Patricia Duffin

First days at work

Factory Floor Fable

I remember, when I was eighteen, getting a job working in a packing factory. I had to be there for eight o'clock on the first day. My cousin also was starting work at the same time as me.

It was a cold day and when I arrived, there were ten other people who were to start work that day.

I waited for a short while and then a lady came to see everyone. She was wearing a white overall and a hair net. She gave everyone the same uniform plus the hair net! She then took myself and all the other people to our work stations. I was put with my cousin so that was not so bad.

I felt uncomfortable because I did not know anyone and no-one was friendly (thank God my cousin was there). It was a big factory with lots of conveyor belts. I was working on a conveyor belt putting thousands of tiny plastic chickens into boxes. You could not move or sit down, you had to ask to go to the toilet (I didn't like that). At 10.40 it was teabreak, by this time I needed a drink as it was hard work. I got to the canteen and I got a cup of tea and lit a cigarette but I did not get time to finish them. A bell rang and I had to get back to the conveyor belt. You were not allowed to drink while working.

I was not fast at packing. I could not pick the chickens up off the conveyor belt quick enough because it was going too fast and they were so small. 12 o'clock came and it was dinner time. I was hungry. My cousin and I went to a cafe. We felt we had to rush our dinner down and we were wondering if we should go back because it was so horrible. We said "It's only the first day, let's see how we go."

When we got back from our dinner we were the only ones left to return. All the other people who started that morning did not come back.

Anyway, in the afternoon, I was put on packing teabags.

I was shattered, I felt like I was going to drop. They got their money's worth out of me!

4.30 came, home-time. I thought, "Great." I went back to my cousin's for tea and when we got there we both felt like crying. It was terrible and we decided not to go back.

I felt like I was treated like a machine. The hard work did not bother me. It was long hours for so little money and I thought, "You will have to pay me a lot more money to go back there." And the people was not friendly either.

I put all this down to experience - not to go for a job in a factory again - not my cup of tea. If I had to make a choice - I would rather clean toilets.

Dawn Gill

About the author

Dawn Gill

I work as an admin assistant which I enjoy. I came to adult education to improve my English. I had very little confidence about my writing before I joined the course. Since starting the class it has helped me in my job and has given me a lot of confidence. I wrote a short piece of course work and my tutor decided to send it to Gatehouse. Before I joined adult education I would never have been able to write anything like this. I feel this is a big achievement.

My first day at work

The morning had arrived, my first day at work. My interview had seemingly gone fine at a shoe shop with a man called Mr. Baker.

"See you early Monday morning," he said, shaking my hand. That was Friday. The weekend flew so quickly, what with buying new clothes and having my hair done.

"No breakfast for me, just a cuppa, mum."

Mum just smiled and said, "You'll be alright."

"Yeah," I said, not really believing it.

It was cold outside, waiting for the bus and I felt ill. My head was banging and my heart was doing over-time. One last look at myself in the shoe-shop window before I walked in there.

"Yeah, you look alright, they'll never know," I thought to myself.

As I walked in, Mr. Baker welcomed me, and pointing to a girl said, "Susan will show you where to put your coat, and she'll show you around."

Walking to the back of the shop, a lady in her fifties walked by, "That's Rita." Susan said.

"Hi" I said.

"Nice to meet you," she said, walking past me. Eh, my heart was somehow making it hard for me to hear.

"Right," Susan said, "this is where your coat and bag goes and this is the staff room, also the stock room."

The smell of leather was so strong.

"First, you must learn where everything is."

I looked round. "God, how can I ever remember where everything is?"

Susan said "You'll be alright. I've worked here for ten years and I can still remember my first day."

I just wanted to stand there and cry. There were thousands of shelves. All seemed full of all the same shoes but different colours. Susan pointed to the boxes of shoes. "They're all coded. Don't worry." she said.

I looked round again at all the boxes. All the names or something was wrote on them. "No," I thought, "I can't do this job." I just stood there and cried.

Mr. Baker came into the stockroom to see what all the noise was about.

"I'm very sorry," I said, "but I can't do this." He just smiled a warm smile, "Have a cup of tea with me. You'll be alright."

I sat having a tea when he said, "You've got the brain and heart for this job."

I smiled and said, "No, I can't do it."

"Oh, yes, you can," he said. "Come on, I'll show you." and we walked to the stockroom.

STAFF

"All them boxes of shoes. Right, go and bring me a shoe off any shelf in the shop, and bring it to me."

I did this and gave him the shoe.

"What colour is this shoe?" he said.

"Black." I said.

"Right, look inside the heel of the shoe. What number does it say?"

"814 - 600".

"Right." he said. "Look at this row of boxes. Look at the number on them 800, 801, 802, 803 etc. They're all number coded," he said. He put his hand on my shoulder and said, "You can do it."

I just smiled, "Great" I thought.

Within twelve months I was relief manageress at different shops, covering for a short period if someone was poorly. The shops were in Liverpool, Sale, and Manchester. I ended up manageress by accident. Again, I was thrown in at the deep end - but that's another story

Vicki Seddon

About the Author

Vicki Seddon

I live in Manchester and come to Newton House adult education centre. I've got three children. I'd been to a Gatehouse book launch and Margaret, my tutor, said they wanted pieces of work for another book about working days. I wrote this piece because it amazed me how it happened to me. It wasn't that hard to write. It isn't that hard to put it right with help. You do need help but it isn't that hard with a good English teacher.

Leaving home for work

The Immigrant

Hello, this is something I have been putting off for a long time - for the simple reason, where do I start? Well, as the man says, at the beginning. I'll go back as far as I can. I was born in the remote district of Craigtown, Carndonagh, Co. Donegal, Eire, of the parents Andy and Nora Farren. There were eleven of us altogether, but sad to say, three died. I had great fun growing up in Ireland. I was very spoiled to six years of age because two babies died between me and Gerard so that left me the baby for a long time. I started school at six years of age (which I didn't want to go to). Do you know why? We lived next door to the school, which was a pain at that time.

I left school at thirteen years and six months and got an apprentice job with my older brother in a cabinet making workshop. Well, sad to say, I didn't finish that. I stayed there for eighteen months, then I went working for a big farmer by the name of Charlie Scott. He was alright, but a savage to work for. I was with him for a couple of years. Mind you, I had a good time as I enjoyed farming. There was nothing nicer than a few days up in the hill, footing* turf. That was our job during our summer holidays and also in the evening when we got home from school.

**Turf, or peat, is dug out of bogland and used as fuel. Footing takes place about ten days after cutting when the peats are built up so the wind can get through them to dry.*

This brings me up to another time...

I am seventeen years and six months and ready to leave home for the first time and my brother Dannie is home on holidays from Scotland. I will tell you the truth - I had mixed feelings. I can still see my mother breaking her heart crying at that time. I didn't know what all the fuss was about. We went up to Derry and got a boat to Scotland. It was a couple of nights after that I realised what it was like to be away from home. It takes a bit of getting used to, being away from home when you are so young and never away from home and family before. It is hard for a country lad; as everybody knows it is a different way of life in the Big City. But I was not too bad as I had a lot of uncles and aunts in Scotland. My uncle John put me to work straight away, so I was lucky in that sense. This was in Dumbarton. I stayed there for a year or so, then we were transferred up the north to Fort William to build a big warehouse.

This brings me up to Christmas. Let me tell you one thing, it was not my choice to leave home. It was the want of employment in Ireland that forced me as an exile to roam far away from home and my family. But let's go back to Scotland. I am going home for my first holiday. I am all excited going home to see the rest of my family. Mother was ever so glad to see me. Mind you I don't blame her! The first thing I did was to give my parents fifty pounds. That was a lot of money then. Mother always said it was the best Christmas we ever had.

I met a few of the lads in Manchester and got a job with a man called Mick Coffey. That was in 1965. Big Mick, he was a giant of a man. He had three or four men working for him at the time, laying gas mains. He would go in the pub of a summer evening after work, it was no bother to him to drink ten pints of bitter and come out in the morning as fit as a fiddle. He was some man. He went on to become a managing - director of a very big company.

I started going to a few old dances here and there. It was not long after that I met a beautiful girl called Eileen Burke.

And on the first day of April 1967 we got married. It was a nice sunny morning. I can remember it well, standing outside St. Thomas' church waiting for her to come... I thought she would never come. It felt like a week but it was all worth it. I will tell you, she looked a picture in her long white dress. We didn't have a big fancy function as we couldn't afford it. Mind you, it was not the 'in thing' like now.

Next year, our son Seamus was born - we were over the moon and in 1970 our second son Eugene was born. He was born a blue baby and had to have all his blood changed. The doctor advised us not to have any more children but that is the way things go.

To be honest, I had a great time in Manchester, they are a great friendly lot of people. In 1966 I met a fine man by the name of Malua Burke. He was a first cousin of Eileen. Myself and him became great friends but sad to say he died in 1993. It broke my heart to see him go! Mind you, I think it didn't do him any good to see me when I had the stroke in January 1990. But, thank God, I lived to tell the tale, although it was touch and go with me. That is why I got another chance back at education. If anybody had told me I would be writing a project or sitting in front of a computer six years ago, I would have laughed at them. I didn't know what one looked like, let alone try to work one.

I'll tell you how it all came about. You see Karen Lewis, my first tutor, was down at the Frank Taylor Centre one day. She asked me if I would be interested in coming on a course in English and computers. I said "Yes, please." It was the best thing I could have done. It has helped me a lot. It has given me a lot of confidence plus the fact that you make a lot of friends and meet plenty more new people.

Seamus Farren

About the author

Seamus Farren

I came into adult education due to the fact that I had a stroke in 1990. So, I decided that I had to do something instead of sitting in the house all day, every day. Karen, my tutor, got us to do an essay and she was very impressed with it. She decided that it should be sent in to Gatehouse as they were looking for a selection of working lives. I didn't go to school long but I've got a great gift of the gab!

I would like to dedicate this writing to my wife, Eileen, and my two sons, Seamus and Eugene, for all the support that they showed me through my illness.

Taking the heat

I came to England from Jamaica when I was 33 years old. My first job was a rubber moulder at Blackfriars Rubber Company. When I started I met a good friend. His name was Noel Sanster and he taught me to run the press.

The presses are different sizes, some large, some small. These presses make jobs for moulding. The jobs are all made of rubber and are used for trucks, cars and are very good in pumps. Some presses had five levers and some had four. When you sent the presses up, you used the low pressure lever and the high pressure lever together.

This would bump the mould and get the job good and get rid of blisters.

If I got a big blister on the job I make in the press, I pricked it with a sharp wire needle and put it in the mould for fifteen minutes, instead of the usual thirty, to cure the job.

The number one man was called Tom Murphy. In the beginning he was a hard man but we became good friends and I was his right hand man. He told me that his brother was the director and said because he swore so much, he must be the devil. Murphy liked to sack men, he even sacked his own uncle because he was not quick on the job. He used to watch the men, and then when they went to the toilet, he would ask me if they were any good.

After eight years, the company sold out to British Vita. Tom Murphy did not go over there. He sacked four more men and then left.

I went to the new company and met some good friends there. The manager was called John Ridge and he was a nice man. But over there they paid no bonuses, and we went back to working twelve hours a day, and we did that for ten years.

I went to hospital for an operation on my knee and I was off work for one year. Then I went back in the Banding Department. I was one of three people painting rings for the men in the press shop. I spent four years in there and then I went back to the press shop when my leg was strong enough.

Then we moved to Ashton to make one large press shop there. My friend, Eric Down, moved there with me which was good because we'd been together for so long. I went to work in the laboratory making small parts for cars and I stayed there until they lost the order. So then I was back in the press shop again and that's where I stayed until I retired in 1988. I enjoyed it because I met some good friends and some good managers. I would have liked to have carried on longer.

Winston Morris

About the Author

Winston Morris

I am writing about myself, what I am doing now. My work is to go on the ministry as a Jehovah's Witness. From house to house we go and tell people what we know. The Bible clearly explains God's will for mankind and the step he is taking to accomplish it.

Coming to the class in Longsight Library helped me a lot. I've been coming to the class five years now. I get along very good with the teachers, all nice and friendly. I have no intention to stop. I started writing about my working life when Barbara asked us. I glad when I get the opportunity to be a part of the class. It's very handy to me, just twenty minutes walk to come up, and everybody very friendly.

Working women from other countries

Women and work in Bosnia

In Bosnia
when there was socialism,
men and women had jobs.
When I was in Bosnia
I worked in a large company
involved with export and import.
My job was that of a head chef.
I cooked for up to 700 people a day.
I worked on a shift rota.
I worked in a very big kitchen.
There were huge cookers,
pots, sinks and utensils.
Everything was huge.

Every day the meal was freshly cooked.
Everybody has free food.
Some of the preparation
was done by another person,
like peeling onions and potatoes.
I was responsible
for all the orders and budgeting.
It was a very, very, hard
and stressful job
especially having to give accounts every day.

At the moment,
in England,
I am not working.

If I want a job
I need to improve my English.
Or if I go to the doctor, post office, anywhere else.
I come to classes at Hulme Centre.
I am speaking better.
I am learning words.
I am more happy than sitting at home.

Dudiya Zilic

About the author

Dudiya Zilic

My life in Bosnia was nice but I came to England because war started. Qaisra, my tutor, often put us together from different countries and she wanted to hear about our culture, custom, women, marriage, divorce. We often spoke with Qaisra and she had to write quickly. She said, "How was your job in Bosnia?" and I told her.

Working for British Rail

I worked with British Rail for twenty seven years. In that time I worked myself up to be a chargewoman. It was a big responsibility. I was in charge of five people in the carriage-cleaning department.

There was one day I will never forget. My inspector was not pleased with the job. He didn't think the carriage was clean enough, so he sent me to go and get it right. I sent one of my workmates to go and get it right. Then when I thought she'd finished, I went and told the inspector it was okay, never knowing she was still on the train. He blew his whistle and the train set off, and my friend ended up at Stockport station. It could have been worse. I got a real telling off from my boss. We never got on, he was a real bad inspector to me and my workmates.

I was born in Jamaica. I worked for 32 years in this country and also raised four children. It wasn't a bed of roses. I had to get up at five in the morning. I didn't like getting up at that time but I did it to suit my family. When I came home I had the family to look after: the shopping, the cooking, the cleaning and washing. My friend helped me with the children. She worked evenings and I used to give her my house key so she could bring my kids back before she went to work.

One day, I forgot to give her the key, so she phoned

me at work. I just panicked. I picked up my bag and went home. I forgot to tell my inspector. The next day when I went back to work, he sent me home and I was suspended for two days without pay. I felt real bad about that. Then, after two days, I went back to work and I think my inspector was feeling guilty. He came up to me and said, "Let bygones be bygones, let's be friends again," and everything was all right after that.

When I used to work it was good fun because I used to meet the public and I enjoyed that. Now that I am not working, I am so glad for this class because it help me to read and write. I can meet people and talk with them, it means a lot to me.

Mable Reeder

About the author

Mable Reeder

When I was seven my mother took sick and had to go to hospital. Two months later she died.

So I grew up with my big sister. She didn't send me to school. I had to stay at home and look after her children.

When you lose your mother at the age of seven, you lose part of your childhood.

I didn't bother about reading and writing. I never thought I would come to England and start a family and have to work to look after them.

My friend who came to England with me went to night school and now she is a nurse. But I just couldn't do that. I was too tired at the end of a hard day's work. So I wasn't able to get such a good job.

Now that I am retired, I am glad of the chance to go to classes, to make up for what I lost when I was young.

When I first started the class I couldn't write very well but now I can write letters to my friends and family and I have more confidence.

Independent Woman

I live in Manchester.
Three years ago
I worked in a knitwear factory.
I had worked there for fifteen years.
The factory closed suddenly
and I was made redundant.

It was then
that I started my catering business
at home.
I started to make Indian snacks
like samosas, bombay mix, pakoras
and some Indian sweets.
Slowly the business grew.

At first, I started to sell to my friends.
Then to a wider community
by word of mouth.

At the beginning, I had small orders.
Then they increased in size and number.
I began to supply my snacks
and full meals
to colleges
and wedding parties in a hotel
and for religious festivals
like Diwali, the Hindu Festival of Light.
At the moment I am very busy.
I cook for one hundred and fifty people.

Sometimes three hundred.
I still work from home.
I get very tired but I love my work.

I am used to running this business.
I just wish I had started earlier.

Champaben Popat

About the author

Champaben Popat

In my spare time I come to Hulme Centre to improve my English. I have now gained enough confidence to speak to people and meet teachers. Before, I was very sad, "How can I talk...?" But when I came here and I met Qaisra* I found that the world has so many good things. I found out very good things here. Before, my life was very sad because each morning, seven o'clock in the dark, I went to a factory. It was dark when I came home. There was not any social life but when I came here I met many new people. This centre has changed my life. Before, I didn't know how to write, "How can I read?" But when I came here, especially when I met Qaisra, then I found out something good. Before, I was scared to go out but when I came here I got the confidence to go out. Now I also help at the temple.

** Her tutor*

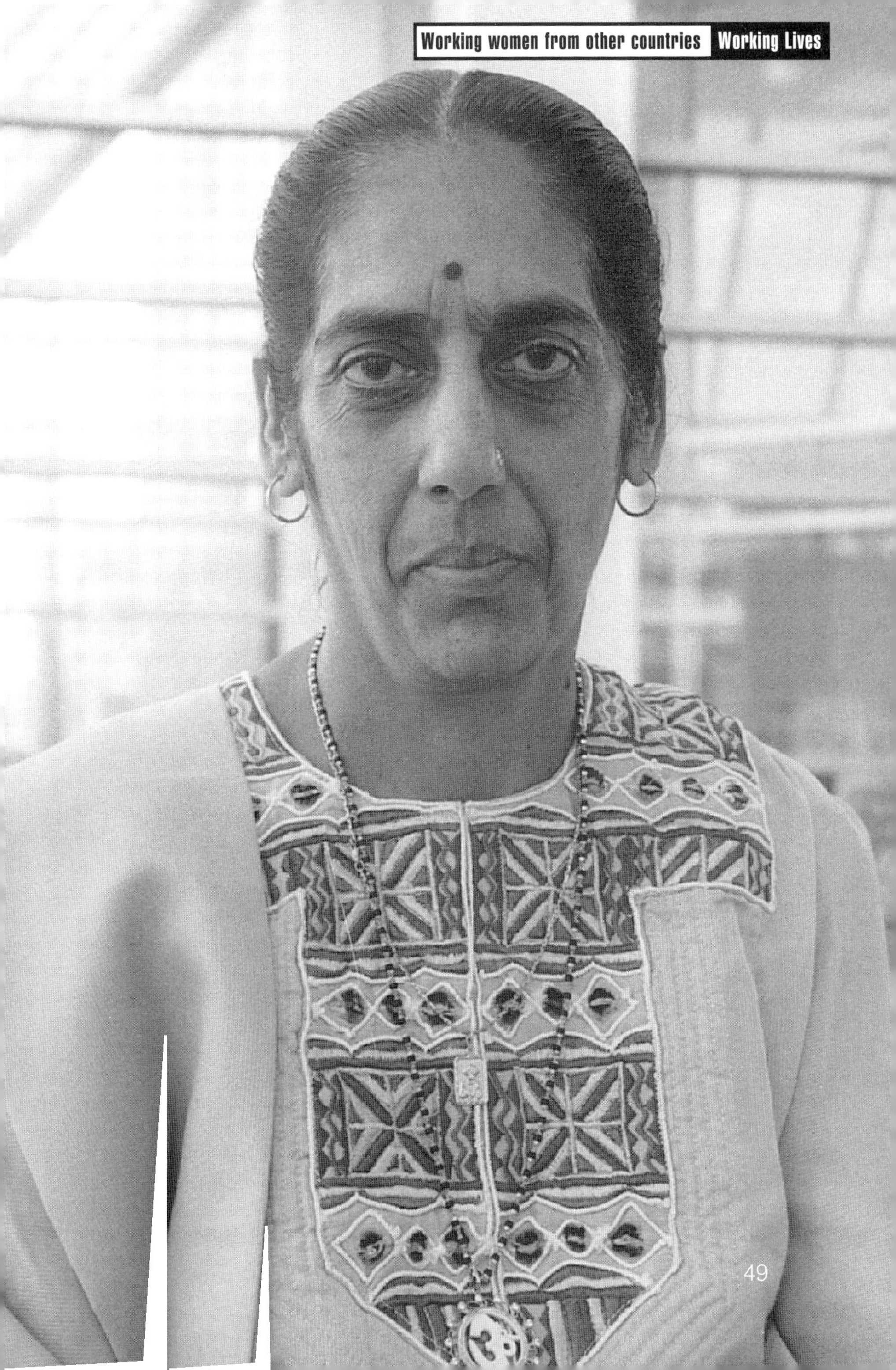

Job after job

All My Working Life

First job

I left school at fifteen and started work at a clothing warehouse in Ardwick. It was called James Stewarts. It had its own tailoring department where they made ladies and gents made-to-measure suits and coats, as well as clothes for their own showrooms. I worked in the ladies' tailoring department as a machinist. It was a very good firm to learn your trade in, as you were taught the tailoring trade right through, from the cutting room to going out to the customer. You were shown all the hand sewing as well as the machining. When you had finished your training there, you were able to get a job at any tailors.

The only thing was that while you were training they did not pay good wages. But we could work in the show room to make up our wages on a Saturday morning and at holiday times when they were busy. We also had a good social life there. We were given a staff outing to Blackpool every summer. The firm would hire a train for the day and the whole warehouse would close for the day and everyone went to Blackpool: bosses, travellers, show room staff, office girls, and workroom staff. The train would leave Manchester at about 9am. Before we arrived at Blackpool we were all given tickets for the pleasure beach where we spent the day doing what we wanted. Then at 6pm we all made our way to the Winter Gardens, where there was an evening dinner and dance held in the ballroom for us. There was a lot of competition between the girls from the office and showrooms, and the girls from the workroom, as to who could be better dressed, as the showroom and office girls thought they were better than the girls in the workroom. I think the girls from the workroom won as we were able to make our own and they were better made.

Being a mother

I worked as a machinist until after I was married and I had my family. This was when I took on the role of a mother. This was what was expected of you then, because if you had a family it was a mother's job to stay at home and look after them. Being a mother then wasn't an easy job as you had to be able to turn your hand to most jobs. You had to be a house-keeper, a cook, an accountant, an odd job man, in fact anything that had to be done, you had to do it. It wasn't easy, as we didn't have a lot of money to spare as there was only one wage coming in. I didn't have all the modern labour saving things that the young mothers today have. I didn't have a washing machine. I didn't have hot water, except for the hot water geyser in the kitchen. We didn't have disposable nappies then. It was terry nappies, washed in the sink and boiled in a small boiler on the gas cooker. There was no bath and we only had an outside toilet that was at the bottom of the yard. I think of all the jobs I have had, being a mother is one of the most demanding jobs there is, as you are expected to work 24 hours a day, 7 days a week and 52 weeks a year, without a day off.

I used to make dresses for my own girls. Being a machinist, it was easy for me and I enjoyed making them. We didn't have any holidays, just the odd days out. Even then it was up early, make sandwiches, pack a bag with spare things for the younger ones.

Back to work

As the children grew up, I went back to work. My first job was in a shop in town. Later on, I was able to get a job as a dinner lady at the local school. After a time, I was asked if I would like to move in to the nursery as an assistant over the dinner time. I really enjoyed working with the younger children. It was while working in the nursery that I found that I was expecting my seventh child.

So once again, I was back to just being a wife and mother. This time it was easier as I did have a modern home and all that goes with a modern home. The other children were growing up and the older ones were working.

When Robert was old enough to go to school I went back to work. I wasn't able to get my old job back in the nursery, but I was asked if I would take a job at the special school across the road. This was Crosby

Meadow school. The children all had special needs and some were physically disabled. My job there was a dining room assistant. Whilst I was working there I also took on the job of escort on the bus that takes autistic children to and from another school. Working with these children can be very rewarding as they can be so loving, but at times they can be very naughty.

Looking back

Looking back on my working life, it has been spent looking after children. I have retired from Crosby Meadow now after working there for fifteen years, but still have my job as the escort.

Rita Norton

About the author

Rita Norton

I am a mother and grandmam. I work with children with special needs, as an escort on the school bus. I wanted to improve my English so decided to enrol at my local evening centre. I was given a lot of help and encouragement by the tutor, Jo Martin. She persuaded me to take my GCSE English which to my surprise, I passed. I had enjoyed the course and like writing. So, when they started the creative writing class it was my chance to carry on writing. It was Jo that asked me if I would like to write a piece on working lives for Gatehouse.

Hard Times

I started work at Henriques Dress Factory in 1965. It was in Pollard Street, Ancoats. I was taught the job of packing. My room was on the top floor of the building, and my window overlooked the Co-op Society.

The factory had three floors. The top floor was Packing and Labelling. We had a machine for addressing labels and I used that. The middle floor was the Machine Cutting Department and Pressers, it was very noisy in there. On the ground floor was the Dispatch Department and Canteen.

In my department I had a small room where I made up my boxes for packing. I had a large table with piles of cardboard and tissue paper. I used to put the dresses in tissue paper before placing them in the boxes.

It was a large concern and sometimes buyers came in and some of the staff modelled the dresses. Sometimes we got returns, and these and other imperfect items were put on the rails, and we were allowed to buy them at cost price.

Our boss, the owner, was Jewish and he would come into the departments in a great hurry. I don't think he ever walked anywhere. Our forelady was called Frances. She was very kind and helped me a lot. Her job was to size the dresses. This made it easy for the packers because it meant we each had only one size to pack.

I found the job very interesting, and I learned a great deal. I was very sorry when I had to give it up. I started having blackouts because I have epilepsy and would have to leave my work and go and sit down.

Frances was very good to me but the foreman decided it was unsafe for me to be there. He was afraid I might fall down the stairs, so I was asked to leave. I had a few days off and then I got a letter to say I was finished.

I was unemployed for a while. Then I had another job packing scents, face powder, tablets, cough medicine, and cough sweets. This didn't work out because my skin was affected.

By now my illness was beginning to get rather bad so my doctor advised I give up the idea of working. I took over looking after my mam and the house and the shopping, the cooking, the cleaning and the washing. This is a hard job in itself. But I am glad that I can do it, and I'm much better now.

Esther Ann Deay

About the author

Esther Ann Deay

My first encounter with the adult education class held at Longsight Library was about 1982. A friend asked me if I would like to go and see for myself what it consisted of. I was introduced to my first tutor. She asked me what I would like to do. I explained to her that I could not write or read very well. She gave me a paper, "See what you can do with that." Of course, made a mess of it but the tutor said, "Don't give up. You can do it and in time you will." How true. After a lot of heartache and bad work which I used to tear up, my tutor told me, "Don't do that, you will only learn by your mistakes." From then on I really got down to studying and I am most grateful to the tutors of our class for the help they are giving me.

Yes, the adult education at Longsight Library is a very good thing. In my case, I owe them many thanks because they gave me confidence in myself and the other students in the class seem to be coming along pretty well. I thought I would never get into it when I first came. Now I enjoy it more and look forward to Tuesday afternoon.

Fluff, Muck and Oil

In the mill

A million years ago, (in 1955) when I was very young, my mother put me in the mill. I had no choice in the matter. She wanted money and I couldn't read or write very well. There was nothing I could do. I didn't want to go in because it was hard work and at 15 years of age you don't want that. I'll never forget the first time I went in the mill, the day I started work. I never knew there was so much noise. It was that bad I kept on putting my hands over my ears. In them days they had no ear plugs to protect your ears, no safety at all. You just had to get on with it or get outside. I was naive, very quiet and some of the women was very frightening. They used to shout at you and if you had done anything wrong, it was a nightmare. They would send for you from the warehouse. You had to go and see what you had done wrong. It was so degrading. There would be faults on the material what you had made by accident. That seemed to give them the right to talk to you like you were a child. They used to tell you that a few years ago you would have had to pay for every fault you had made. It was humiliating. I just didn't know what to do. I couldn't run anywhere, I had to stand there and say nothing.

The woman that was teaching me how to weave seemed very old but knew everything there was to know about weaving. She had six looms, very big machines. They were Lancashire looms which stopped every five minutes so you had to be quick setting them on, putting in another shuttle with new weft in it. Every machine had a clock on it so every time the shuttle went across the loom, it was one pick. At the end of the week you would count how many picks you had on the clock and you would get paid for whatever you had made. It was very hard work and very dirty. By the time you went home you were full of fluff: up your nose, in your hair, everywhere. But I did it for years, on and off. Obviously, as time went by, the machines got better and bigger. I got laid off once or twice. Mills kept on closing, so I had to learn something else as I needed the money. I had two children to look after. Yes, I did have a husband, but that is another story.

Engineering

I went into Engineering, went to work for the Government ROF (Royal Ordinance Factory). You had to have a vetting to get in there but once you got in, you had a job for life. Again, it wasn't easy. You had so many components to make in an hour and you got paid by what you had made. They put me on a capstan (a big lathe). I had never seen one of these before. I thought I would never do it but like anything else, eventually, you master it and then you seem to get cocky and that is when you make mistakes. We wasn't allowed to make mistakes as we were making guns, fuses, and things all to do with the Army. So they had to be 100 per cent, not 99 per cent. By the end of the day you were covered in oil, all over your hair, clothes, arms, everything, but now and again we had a laugh, and that made it all worthwhile. My money went down and by this time my children had gone but I now had a house to pay for.

Welding

So I tried another job in the next town. Twelve hours a day it was, making petrol tanks. I had to weld them, solder them and put them in a cold water tank to see if they had any holes in them. Summer was all right but in the winter you had to go in and break the ice on top of the tank, then put your hands and arms in it for five minutes. In the end, it got too much for me.

When I look back, I'm only glad my daughter hadn't to go in the mill or engineering. I wouldn't want her to have to go through what I did, and all because I couldn't read and write.

If I'd had a bit of education I might have found another job. I'd have liked to have done something like drawing or design.

Pearl Dewhurst

About the author

Pearl Dewhurst

I live with my daughter and my grandaughter which I love very much. I go to school twice a week to learn English which has given me much more confidence to try most things. I also go to the craft classes where I am making a patchwork quilt. The rest of the week I go to a friend's house to help her with a few things around the house, clean, make dinner and have a chat about things, which I find very rewarding.

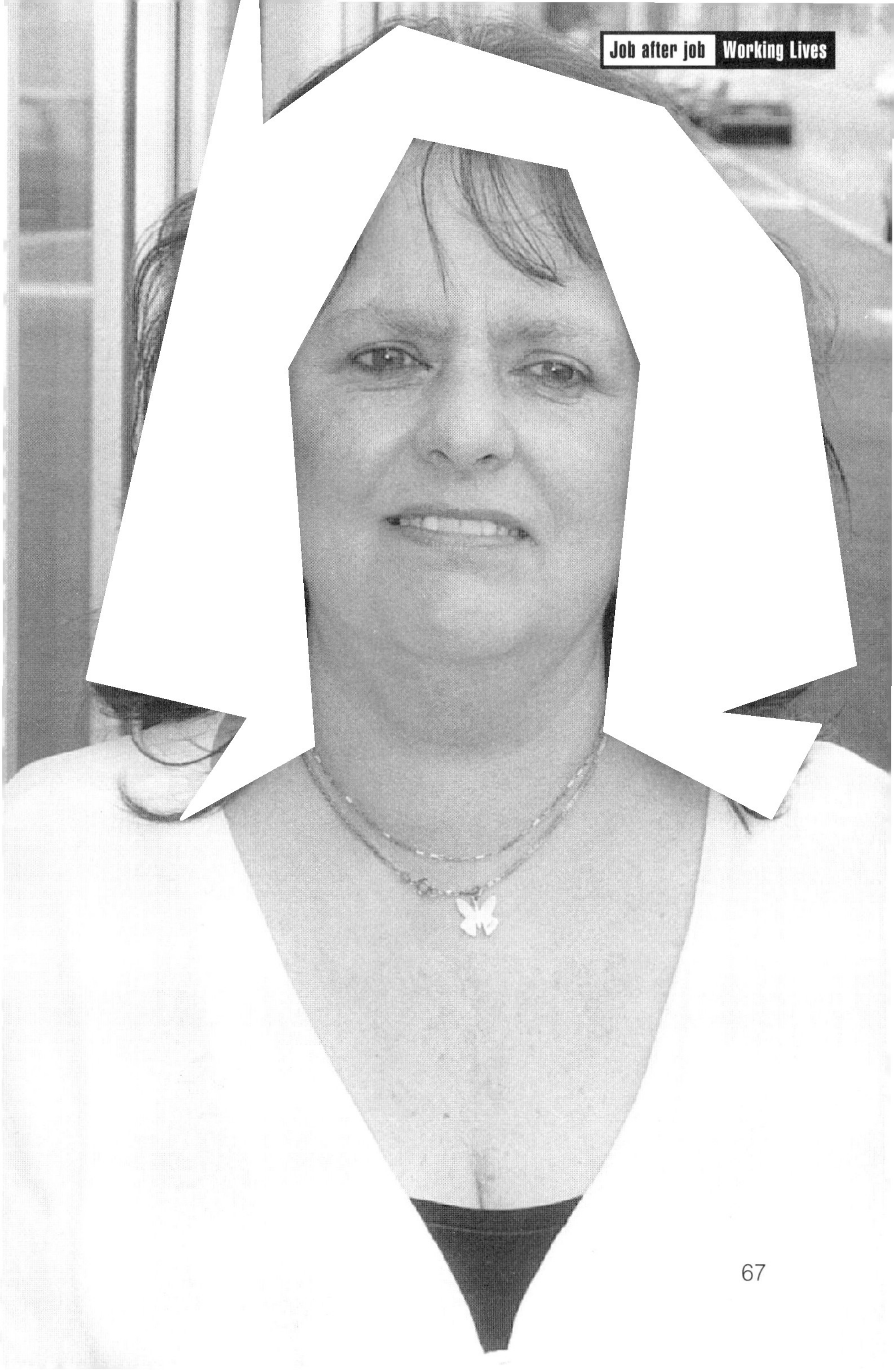

Joining the elite

It was the summer of 1939. Neville Chamberlain, the Prime Minister, had returned from Munich, waving his peace treaty, claiming, 'Peace in our time.' I was 16 and on the dole. Two summers before, on leaving school at 14, I had become an apprentice dressmaker. Now, war clouds hung menacingly. Customers panicked and cancelled their orders. They were to regret this when clothing coupons were eventually introduced. My boss had no alternative but to stand me off.

After five weeks waiting to be called into work, my mother said, in her practical Yorkshire way, "I can't be doing with this. Get yourself down to the Co-op and get yourself a job. Men are being 'called-up.'* There are jobs going."

I got onto my bicycle and got myself down the Co-op. I had no appointment. I just walked into the shop, asked to see the Manager and was shown into his office.

This large man in his fifties, with pale freckled face, fading red hair and moustache, sat behind his desk, smoking. Above him hung, in decorative lettering like a religious text, were the words, "It is better to remain silent and be thought a fool than to speak out and remove all doubt."

** to join the armed forces*

I cannot recall much of the interview. I remember the manager quickly jotting down some simple questions such as, "How many pennies in a pound?" and leaving me to answer them. "Start on Monday," I was told.

So it was that the Second World War broke out on Sunday 3rd of September and the following day I became the Junior Drapery Assistant at the Pocklington, East Yorkshire branch of the Co-operative Wholesale Society under the manageress, Winnie.

I had joined the elite. Co-op assistants considered themselves the cream of shop assistants. As a first year dressmaker's apprentice I had earned five shillings a week. At the Co-op, my first wage was fifteen shillings.

The Drapery Department was above the Grocery Department.

The Co-op sold only their own brands of drapery and shoes. Much of the stock, such as men's overcoats, brace and bib overalls, khaki warehouse coats, woollen combinations, vests and liberty bodices, were stored in brown paper parcels.

I was taught to make a slip knot, pull out a loop, slip it round a parcel, pull it up tightly, bring the string round and tie it in a half bow for easy opening.

Our department gleamed. Winnie had a passion for polishing. Every Friday, every parcel, every shoe box and every fixture was dusted. Winnie and I took up and scrubbed the rubber mats advertising

'Wheatsheaf Shoes' and 'Pelaw Shoe Polish', got down on our knees and polished every inch of floor. The two chairs in front of the counter for customers use and the counter front was polished. The floor was kept buffed with a dry mop for the rest of the week.

'Drapery department,' was an umbrella term covering many lines. Great rolls of linoleum stood in a niche against the boots. When full, we could not manhandle them. A man from the grocery department was called to help. The roll was dropped to the floor, pattern downwards, the required yards marked out and numbered on the wrong side and rolled up to touch the main roll. Both were turned over and the lino cut along the pattern on the right side.

Binding coconut matting was the only job I really disliked. It was a loathsome task. Winnie and I sat on high stools with the matting over a small side counter and stitched with strong thread. Folding the binding and stitching through two layers did not work. Each edge of binding had to be stitched separately.

During my first week working at the Co-op, I was alone in the department when a small boy came to the counter and said, "My Grannie says, please can she have two barrows for our new baby?" I knew nothing about babies and sent him to the hardware department, thinking such a toy was an odd gift for a new baby. Later, the Grannie came in and explained that the barrows she wanted were small flannel baby garments. My knowledge of baby garments and our stock was extended that day.

Many families in the town and surrounding villages in the catchment area were clothed on the Mutuality Club. Customers came into the shop, paid one shilling*, bought £1's worth of goods and paid off at one shilling a week. That £1 went a long way. It would buy a pair of corduroy working trousers, two union working shirts, or perhaps short sleeved woollen vests or some boots. A cloth cap for one and nine, braces for a shilling and the odd red cotton spotted handkerchief to make up the odd coppers.

On Monday mornings I set out on my bicycle and went for the day on the Club round, collecting customers' shillings. I went to all areas of the town, rich and poor alike. I went into their homes and they became friends.

During those years on my rounds I saw my customers' lives change. Pretty curtains were exchanged for black cotton or sateen. The more artistic embroidered them with crinoline ladies watering hollyhocks under trellis arches. I saw their iron railings uprooted and taken to make ammunition, and kitchen tables replaced by ugly metal air-raid shelters under which families slept night after night. Husbands and sons went to war and photographs of soldiers, sailors and airmen appeared on mantelpieces as the women brought up children alone.

There were changes at the shop too. Gradually, most of the young and up to middle-aged male staff was

** Refers to currency in use before 1971*

called-up and women replaced them. Girls went too.

Because of black-out restrictions, fear of falling bombs, rationing, shortages and power cuts our world was turned upside down. Prices went up, and we worked fewer hours to avoid the blackout as much as possible.

1942 dawned. I was 19 and had to register for work of National Importance. I volunteered, joined the WRNS* and working days were never the same again.

Sylvia Rowley

---

* *Women's Royal Naval Service*

About the author

Sylvia Rowley

I was born and brought up in Barmby Moor, a small village in the East Riding of Yorkshire. After my marriage, I moved two miles down the road to the market town of Pocklington. I have a son and a daughter and four grandchildren. During the Second World War I served four years in the WRNS as a cook. For many years I've enjoyed "scribbling a bit". Twelve years ago I moved to Manchester. A big change from life in the country. Although I have settled in the county of the red rose, I still wave my white rose at every opportunity.

Best times

Night shift girls

I was so fed up at home. I decided to go and look for a job. I went and I got this job at Smiths Foods. It was the best time for me, I never had so much fun. The children were very young so I decided to do the night shift. It was hard work but it was what I could do at the time to fit in with the children going to school.

I started at ten o'clock at night and worked until six in the morning. First, I had to put my overall on before I went on to the factory floor. I had to get my chair and put it where I was working and then I got my boxes to pack the crisps in.

I had to put forty-eight packs in a box and they had to be the correct weight. If the box wasn't the right weight, the machine threw it off. Sometimes, one of the girls would put a bad pack in the box. When the machine threw it off we all had a good laugh watching the controller having to rip the box open.

There were sixteen of us working on the conveyor belt and we were all good friends, but my best friend was Iris. Me and Iris used to go in the coat room for a natter and a joke. We had a good laugh together. We were like two golden girls, and all the other girls wanted to know what we'd got up to over the weekend. "Not a lot, girls," we would say, laughing.

It was fun working together, and the saddest part was when we got made redundant because we had to

eparate from each other. I still see some of the girls.
hose times were good times with good memories.

Beryl O'Connor

About the author

Beryl O'Connor

I was born in Jamaica and came to England in 1961. I got a job and I start work and after a while I get married and two years later I have a baby and it was just so. Four years later I went back to Jamaica to see the rest of the family. My husband come from Jamaica too so we go back on holiday. Then I was there again last December and it was fantastic. I hope to go back soon. I am a mother of six children and I also have six grandchildren. I look after my grandchildren some days after school. Coming to England was a good experience. Starting this class has been a good experience for me.

A camera never lies

I often help out in my husband's photographic business. One morning an elderly lady telephoned the studio and asked if we would take a photograph of her dog. I told her that we could fit her in one afternoon later in the week and asked if this was convenient. There was a slight pause, then she said that she couldn't wait that long as there was a bit of a problem. The problem was that her dog was dead and it was going to be buried at a local kennels later that day. The lady only had some snapshots of her dog and she wanted some professional photographs to remember it by. Philip, my husband, agreed to photograph the dog immediately and the lady brought its body to the studio. We had to remove a rather heavy and very dead cocker spaniel from the boot of her car and carry the poor thing into the studio. We placed it in its basket and draped one of its ears over the side. It just looked as if it was peacefully sleeping. When the lady came in to collect the photographs she was very pleased with them but being animal lovers ourselves we didn't have the heart to charge her for them. As she left the studio clutching her treasured photographs Philip turned to me and said, "I hope her husband lives a very long time."

One day a young man came into the studio with a lot of old black and white photographs. It was soon to be his parents' silver wedding and he wanted the photographs copied and enlarged and then mounted in an album as a gift for them.

One of the photographs was of a large group of people and in the group, but at opposite ends, were his mother's parents. He wanted a close-up photograph producing of the two of them together because his mum didn't have one. The album was ready a couple of weeks later and the young man came in to pick it up. He was looking through the album and when he came to the photograph of his grandparents he appeared to be very amused. When he managed to compose himself he explained that his grandfather had tragically lost his left eye in the war and wore glasses with a patch covering one lens. However, when the artist photo-finisher had seen the patch on the original small photograph he thought that it was glare from the sun on the man's glasses, so he had painted an eye in on the enlargement when he was doing some retouching. We sent the photograph back to be retouched again and the old man was none the wiser that he had got his eye back forty odd years after he had lost it.

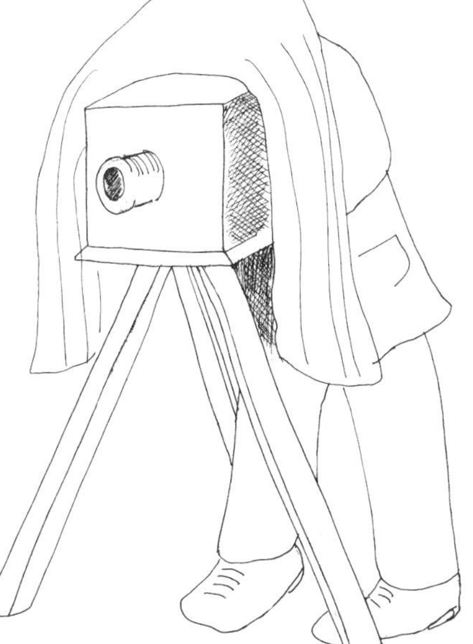

Some people think that all photographers have glamorous and exciting lives. Well, we live in hope!

Linda Green

About the author

Linda Green

I have a son, a daughter and two grown-up stepdaughters and I have been married to Philip for twenty years. My various employments have always entailed a lot of writing but I still felt I needed to improve my punctuation. I enrolled in adult education classes and apart from the desired improvement in my punctuation I have discovered "writing for pleasure". My interests are reading, sewing, do-it-yourself, gardening, photography and travel.

Memories of a mill girl

The happiest days of my life were spent in a mill. They were hard days and the work was very heavy. I started work when I was fourteen years old in 1944. The hours were 5.30am until 10.30am. As I was under sixteen years old, I was only allowed to work so many hours. I had to come back at 1.30pm and work until 5.30pm. The people were very friendly and you soon learned the job. As I was only small, the first job I had was cleaning. The lady who was teaching me, whose name was Annie Cross, did not like cleaning the frames. We had twenty-four frames to clean. So, first I was taught with the frames stopped, then as I got more experienced I had to clean them while they were running. At first, I was scared stiff of Annie as she was a hard taskmaster. If it wasn't done properly, I would have to do it again and again until it was done to her satisfaction. I eventually learned how to do the job and began to like it. Even though it was very dirty and noisy you soon got used to it. In fact, everybody who had worked in a mill could lip read. I got a lot more experienced at doing the job and lip reading.

Then, when I was sixteen I moved up the ladder to learn to be a 'boxtender'. It is a bit difficult to explain and it took a lot of skill. You also made your own wages as every lot of frames had a clock and every so many yards of cotton the clock would register as to the number you had done. Then, at the end of the week, you could reckon how many 'hanks' or yards of cotton you had done to form your wages. As my mother was hard up, like so many families, I could never leave this job as the money was so good. If I had to go to the toilet the frames were left running, six of them, so I didn't lose any money. Soon I was earning £5 per week, which was a lot of money in those days, and I was given only half a crown (12½p) per week spends. As it was sixpence (2p) to go to the pictures and half a crown to go to the dance, my spends did not go very far.

We all worked Saturday morning to make extra money if we had finished our own work early. I used to clean other frames and they would pay me, which my mother allowed me to keep. I sometimes made as much as 6 shillings (30p) with which I bought new clothes, such as blouse and skirt, but it took four weeks' money to buy them.

It really was a cotton mill town, Shaw, and Oldham. Now, all the mills are shut, they're all mail-order places now, them what's not been knocked down. Nowadays, I go to Uppermill in Oldham to look at the museum. It has part of a mill and the old boilers we used, all those years ago. It has been kept like that for memories.

Nora Ashton

About the author

Nora Ashton

I was born in Shaw, a cotton mill town. I was brought up in Shaw but when I was eight or nine there was a coal strike. No coal, no mills. So, my father and my Uncle Elijah, walked to Birmingham and got work there. And we stayed there until we got bombed out. I came back to Shaw then.

When I finished work completely and had no grandson to look after, it was doing my head in. So I came to Newton House Adult Education Centre. It's more fun here - they're a good crowd. I came last year to the history class. I found you could talk to people more. I never thought I was clever enough to write my story. It felt good putting it down. I didn't think it would be interesting to anybody. I thought, "They won't know what I'm talking about!," but Deirdre said, "Put it down, Nora, have a bash! Have a go!"

My Dad

Damp street, damp wind, channelled by those lines of red brick two-up two-down, outside-lav homes. Grey people, bowed by their heavy outside coats, nodded to each other as they passed. Yellow light fell from windows whose curtains had not yet been drawn. One of these two-up two-downs was my home, my security.

School had finished over two hours before and I had, with great eagerness, consumed my chips, fish fingers and peas. The radio filled what empty spaces there were in that small cramped room, with its clutter of five children and two adults. The smell of tripe and onions oozed from the scullery. My mum was preparing my dad's tea.

You should see my dad - silver white head, arms freckled and tattooed. Big Irish man. Irish in mind and face. Oh, and temper too. But strong and safe like some old king who dealt out justice, hard but fair. He would be on his way home now, home from Old Trafford. Trafford Park, whose endless factories grunted and groaned-out their finished wares. My dad was a crane driver. He drove his crane for Metro Viks. To me, and I am sure to others, he was important.

I grab my coat, shouting at the scullery door, "Going to meet Dad."

BUS
STOP

Up the street of uneven flags and glistening cobbles. I turn left, past the corner sweet shop with its enamelled panels advertising the benefits of Capstan Full Strength. Two blocks and I am at the bus stop, the 53 bus stop, whose low wall provides a convenient seat.

Buses big and red, trundle up, and even before they have quite stopped, passengers spew out of the rear. No, not on this one, not on the next or on any of the next five. Worry starts to set in. Is everything OK?

I count cars up to twenty and if the twentieth is black all will be right. Pretty safe bet, as most then were black. I peer up the road and just in view appears the front of a red monster, with its belly full of humans. Will it come to my stop? I can't yet see its number. Will it turn away at the lights leaving me with fallen hope?

No, on it comes, swaying gently from side to side like a boat chugging along to land its cargo. Slowly it draws closer to the kerb. People, mostly men, are already skipping off, darting this way and that to their homes, pulling up the collars of their colourless coats, lunch bags thrown over one shoulder. The bus makes a juddering stop, making those, who have not already, shift feet to regain balance.

I see my dad. He steps down from the bus onto the kerb, his caution due to leg damage caused by one of Hitler's shells. A hero, my dad. A smile lights up his face and he swings his ex-army lunch carrier over my shoulder. It swings round my legs. His arm falls over my shoulder, fingers orange from tobacco. A Woodbine dangles from his lips, blowing red sparks as he speaks.

Overtime had made him late and as I listened, the smell of nicotine, grease and sweat filled my nose. The smell of my dad, safe and nearly home.

Hugh Walsh

About the author

Hugh Walsh

Born Moss Side in 1950 with the shadow of war still lurking in forgotten corners. My dad was from a far off land called Ireland. My mum, Manchester born. Catholicism and the eleven plus my reason for existing. I failed both.

I have always loved words. Maybe because we were late in getting a television. My problem was I could not spell, so school had no interest in me. About three years ago I ended up in a creative writing class where my problem about spelling was dismissed. So I wrote. I do hope you enjoy my writing because that's why I wrote it. I wrote it for you.

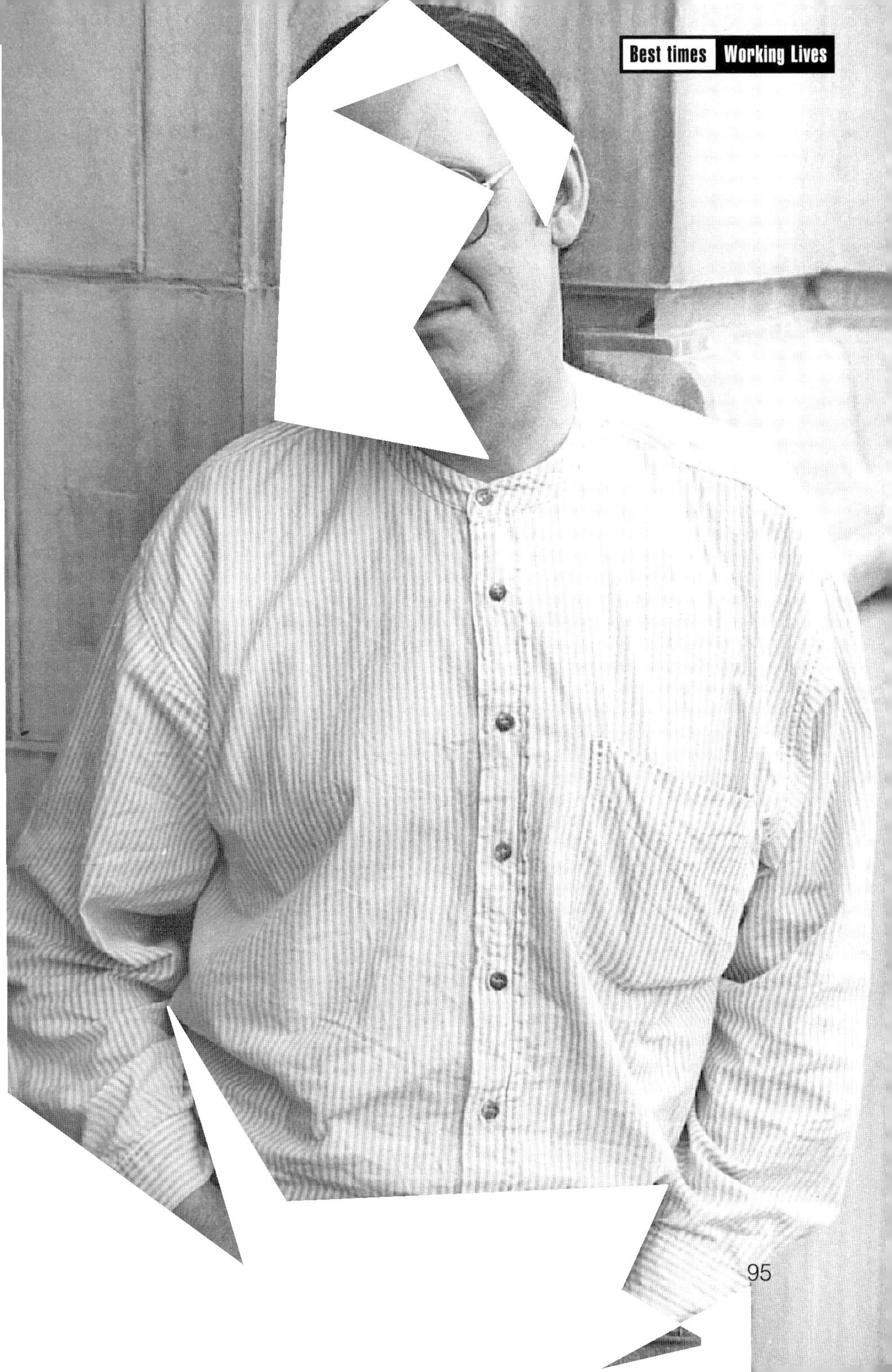

Dedication

To Jean

This is not her real name but for personal reasons she had decided to use a different name.

Unfortunately, due to Jean's sudden death Gatehouse didn't have the opportunity to work on her writing with her for publication. As a result, we have edited her words in order to make them clearer for the reader. We also asked her tutor, Judith Kidd, to explain something of the two worlds that Jean has written about.

Two Worlds

What are two worlds? They are the hearing community and the deaf community. The deaf community has its own culture which is deaf culture. Many deaf people use as their first language British sign language (their own grammatical and visual means of communication). This is different from spoken and written English, and the way deaf people experience the world through their own language is different from hearing people.

The deaf community or club is a second home for many deaf people. They feel at home in the deaf community as isolation is the biggest suffering in the hearing world. The deaf club is a place to share news and be accepted for themselves, It is a place to relax and be at peace with friends who can communicate, who understand each other's culture and needs.

Judith Kidd

Two Worlds

I'm profoundly deaf since birth. I went to a school for the deaf till I was sixteen years old. I haven't got on really well with mixed deaf and hearing people since I was young because I was confused between the deaf and the hearing worlds. Also, I was shy about meeting them. My father and two young brothers could all hear. However, my mother is deaf.

All my life I have been frustrated because I found it too difficult to communicate with my father and my brothers. I know that my father could use sign language because his parents were both deaf. My parents used to lip read to me, to make me feel frustrated. Also, my brothers didn't want to learn sign language.

Anyway, when I left school I was quite happy until I got a new job. I disliked mixing with hearing people when I was the only deaf person. Later, I realised that I wished to return to school. However, I continued to work until the factory closed down. Then, I got a job in a factory where the Welfare for the Deaf knew that two deaf men worked. I worked as a hand finisher. I was happy at work, but did not get on well with hearing people. Anyway, a few months later, my mother joined me at work. I worked there for four years until the firm closed down.

The third job I did was as a shirt presser, with my husband, for a few years until I got pregnant.

I was very happy as a housewife with two deaf boys. However, one problem was that I disliked mixing with the hearing mothers and toddlers group. However, I encouraged my two kids to play with hearing children before they went to the nursery, to give them confidence. My two children got used to mixing with hearing children. It was good for them because I didn't want them to be like me when I was a little girl.

I hadn't returned to work after I was pregnant. However, I had been looking after my husband, who was ill, for four years, until he died. I started to go to the deaf club every week, to improve my skills.Then, two years later, I got a new job making sandwiches. This was a small company. I worked there for fourteen months, then they didn't need me any more. However, I was happy to leave work because I hated working inside four walls without any windows. Also, it was very difficult to communicate with the two ladies and the boss kept his eyes on me constantly. I haven't looked for a job since because at the moment I am looking after my widowed mother.

Now, I would like to look for a new job.

Jean

Gatehouse Books

Gatehouse is a unique publisher

Our writers are adults who are developing their basic reading and writing skills. Their ideas and experiences make fascinating material for any reader, but are particularly relevant for adults working on their reading and writing skills. The writing strikes a chord - a shared experience of struggling against many odds.

The format of our books is clear and uncluttered. The language is familiar and the text is often line-broken, so that each line ends at a natural pause.

Gatehouse books are both popular and respected within Adult Basic Education throughout the English speaking world. They are also a valuable resource within secondary schools, Social Services and within the Prison, Education and Probation Services.

Booklist available

Gatehouse Books
Hulme Adult Education Centre
Stretford Road
Manchester M15 5FQ

Tel: 0161 226 7152

The Gatehouse Publishing Charity Ltd is a registered charity, number 1011042. Gatehouse Books Ltd is a company limited by guarantee, registered number 2619614.